A Pocket Full

Elaine J Jeffrey

A Pocket Full of Hope

Elaine J Jeffrey
2019

No surnames have been included in this book to protect individual's personal privacy.

Copyright © 2019 by Elaine J Jeffrey

All rights reserved. This book or any portion thereof may not be reproduced or transmitted in any form by any means electronic, mechanical, photocopying or otherwise, or used in any manner whatsoever without the prior permission of the publisher.

All correspondence to:

elainejjeffrey@hotmail.com

First Published: 2019

ISBN 978-0-244-81607-0

Dedication

To my husband, sons, family and friends.

Thank you so much.

Without your love, support and patience,

I would have never achieved my dream.

God Bless you all.

Contents

Acknowledgements: ix

Introduction: 1

Chapter 1: This Is Me, My Story, My Journey   3

Chapter 2: My Bumpy Booby-Trapped Journey   11

Chapter 3: The Start of My Lumpy Bumpy Trip   14

Chapter 4: Verdict Day   24

Chapter 5: Chemotherapy   50

Chapter 6: Hair Today, Gone Tomorrow   58

Chapter 7: Wig Wham, Thankyou Ma'am   65

Chapter 8: The C Word   70

Chapter 9: Counselling   99

Chapter 10: My Family   101

Afterword: 113

Acknowledgements

Devoted thanks & blessings to Paul, my husband, best friend, soul man and soul mate. With all my fears and doubts, you always believe in me and you are a constant source of encouragement. I am so thankful God brought us together.

Heartfelt thanks to:
My wonderful mum and dad for all their unconditional love, attending all my appointments with me, (even though I am a big girl now) and for always being a constant support.

My loving supportive family and friends who chose to walk the journey with me rather than run in the other direction.

Special Loving Thanks to:
My 3 sons for being such strong solid rocks for their Mother Goose, Birth Giver and Mam.

I have so much admiration for you lads. I am so very proud of you all.

Much love to my stepchildren and grandchildren.

Special thanks to all who helped me through my darkest times.

A Big Thank You to Daniel and Jonathan for their prophecies, Pastor Keith, his wife Avril and all who pray for me even today at FERN church, Haworth, West Yorkshire.

Grateful thanks to Anna and Jonathan for giving me their valuable advice, support, and prayers.

I'm also so grateful to all of you who have been there for me, as I couldn't have got through all this without you.

Your continued support is very much appreciated.

Elaine J Jeffrey

Introduction

My Book

Where do I start?

Book

noun

1.
a written or printed work consisting of pages glued or sewn together along one side and bound in covers.

2.
a bound set of blank sheets for writing in.

Then there is my version...

3.
blank pages, which my aim was to fill with my own cancer journey, in the hope that you may receive something positive from it.

A Pocket Full of Hope

So, go on, make yourself a cuppa, get comfy, and have a read. In my heart I really hope you will enjoy my book and that it will also raise awareness of Breast Cancer to help others.

"If you were born with the weakness to fall, you were born with the strength to rise!"
Rupi Kaur

How true!

Exodus 23:20*
A promise of the lord's presence.
"I am sending an angel before you to protect you on your journey."

Jeremiah 29:11*
"For I know the plans I have for you," declares the Lord, "plans to prosper you and not harm you, plans to give you hope and a future."

"Our backs tell journeys and stories no books have the spine to carry."

Chapter 1

This Is Me, My Story, My Journey...

Owning our own story can be hard, but not as nearly as much as running from it.

"Only when we are brave enough to explore the darkness will we discover the infinite power of light" - Brene Brown

To My Daughter

Wherever your journey in life may take you, I pray you'll always be safe, enjoy the ride and never forget your way back home, I am always here for you.

Love Mum

X

A loving note from my mamma.

I am writing this book to give an insight about my journey including my diagnosis, my faith in God and my fight to reach out of the dark tunnel, emerging into the brighter, lighter side, whilst still learning to be more understanding of my emotional and physical needs.

To write, is having the ability to move people, hopefully to connect with their own emotions.

I have channelled my own cancer experience and learnings into my book, hoping that it helps others on their own paths.

"It's going to be tough, but I'm determined to do it"
Matilda, Roald Dahl

I believe, because of my prophecies, that I have been called to express myself in this creative way, to share my story, and at the same time, guiding you along your own inspiring journey in life.

You never know unless you try.

I have always wanted to write a book but felt that I have never had the right words (or even enough words for a whole book!) nor the confidence to fulfil my wish.

"To believe yourself to be brave, is to be brave, it is the only essential thing." - Mark Twain

So, let me explain, this 'book' started out for my own purpose, it is not exactly a self-promotion, it's just a way to try and heal my mind and body, to save myself, a memoir, to make sense of my own journey and my own emotional rollercoaster, and to get rid of my insecurities and fears of failure.

Yet, if in the process of it, it helps even just one person, then I will say with a huge smile on my face, and with all my heart, "Amen & Thank You God".

Prophecies

Whilst attending church, on different occasions, I had speakers prophesying on a few things to me.
They didn't know anything about me, had never met me, or I them.

Now, I have never told anyone about my dreams, and wishes, yet here they were, telling me so many things, of which one was that they could see many books around me and, wait for it... ME writing a book!

At first, I thought, ha! yeah right! Me?

But then it suddenly hit me, and I thought, wow! ok, well, the message is actually from God and if the lord wants me to write a book then he must have faith in me, as I have faith in him, so, I will try my best to fulfil both his and my wish, all while hoping he will guide me through the process, (as I always get lost, I have no sense of direction at all, ha-ha.) ↑□□□➡□↓□

A Pocket Full of Hope

I want to explain that I believe in God, not because my parents told me to, and even though both my nans encouraged me when I was a little, (both taking me to different churches, confusing for a child!), but in the end the choice was mine alone, because I have experienced his presence and workings in my life.

Praise the Lord.

Now, the only thing I have that no one else has is me, my mind, my voice, my vision, and my story. So, I write only as I can, with the hope that any Cancer Awareness, no matter how short my story, creates a better understanding to anyone who is going through it, either themselves or knows someone who is.

So, if you have ever tried to write a book, you know how it goes…

You stare at a blank page for a few minutes, but it feels like hours.

A Pocket Full of Hope

Your mind starts to wander, mine always does, my brain was suddenly blank, it may have been in overdrive, filled with mixed up thoughts that were buzzing around like an angry wasp with a bad attitude, it was all so confusing...

My inspiration said "not today cupcake"
(Tomorrow doesn't look very promising either) then it left me wondering when it would decide to bless me with its presence again...

So, off I went to make yet another Macchiato, & maybe even reach for a biscuit, (while trying to resist the cake), crossing my fingers and hoping they were going to solve the problem...

Hmm, (there was more chance of me only succeeding in putting on weight due to the copious amount of coffee and biscuits, with or without cake, than finishing my first book.)

So, while trying to divert my mental roadblocks, feeling like I was going around and round a roundabout until dizzy, is NOT a good sign, especially when I really needed my mind to be focused...Ha! I am so easily distracted...
Ooh look another biscuit ...

I also needed to be prepared for the first steps to producing (something resembling) a book.

Now, As I mentioned previously, I have always liked the idea of writing my own book but liking and achieving this idea is a very different story!

I then started to worry about "not being an expert!" and was worried I would let my so called 'book' end up in my graveyard of dreams, where my ideas would be buried, and my memory unable to recall where they went, deeply hidden somewhere...

A Pocket Full of Hope

I blame memory loss on four things.
Now what are they?
Oh yeah, I remember…

1. Brain fog, due to the chemotherapy.
2. Being hit on the head 3 times when I was badly attacked.
3. The early menopause.
4. Fatigue.

Talk about mind games, mine likes playing hide and seek!

Allegedly, writers are told to write what they know, yet all I know is that I don't really know that much ha-ha. Help!

Chapter 2

My Bumpy Booby-Trapped Journey

Once upon a time...

It sounds like the beginning of a good story doesn't it?

Well, the jury is out on that one, because I haven't decided if it is a bad story because of the cancer, or a good story because I really am privileged to still be here and to be able to write about it.

Pfft! Of course, it is good, I am alive!

So, are you sitting comfortably? Ok, buckle up, and hopefully you'll enjoy the ride.

Here goes...

A Pocket Full of Hope

February 2013, I divorced after 26 years together. (Not my fault, by the way.)

July 2013, I was diagnosed with Breast Cancer.

October 2013, I spent 3 days packing boxes, attended 2 hospital appointments, moved into a rented house on the Saturday, unpacked and then started my chemotherapy treatment on the Monday.

Looking back, I honestly do not know how I coped with it all!

I can only be truly thankful to my family and friends who helped me.

Let me tell you, while I was ill, my friend Debi helped me enormously by finding me a house to rent. All I had to do was to meet my landlord, view the house, then move in. It was the only house I viewed, and it had the bonus of being on the next street to Debi's house. Good choice I'd say.

Update

We have both moved houses since then, but I will never forget our days as neighbours, as well as crazy friends, through good times and bad, happy and sad, in both our homes, and in the ginnel.

Even today she is still such a kind, considerate, mad, funny, twisted friend. Sorry Debi, but you really are. Lol.

So, Thank you so much, Duchess Debi. ♛

One day my childhood friend Fiona, contacted me to say she had been and had a tattoo done on her wrist, it was a pink ribbon, the emblem for Breast Cancer, for me, to show just how strong I had been through it all.

Thanks Fee, that is certainly a brave thing to do and definitely a permanent reminder!

Chapter 3

The Start of My Lumpy Bumpy Road Trip

It all began on one Saturday in July, the 6th to be precise.

I remembered it had been such a lovely sunny day, yet that evening became darkened with a huge black cloud hanging over me.

Why? you may wonder, because whilst taking a shower, I found a lump.

I wasn't looking for one, but it found me, I wasn't even doing a self-examination.

(Which I cannot emphasize enough to all ladies and gentlemen, how very important it is to check every month.)
(I know, I know, I should have listened to my own advice.)

Anyway, I felt a lump, which had reared its ugly self, right there in my right booby.

So, after many times checking it and hoping each time somehow it would not be there when I checked again, but no, it was always there, it did not disappear, it was an unwelcome squatter, never getting the message to vacate my body, it just stayed making itself right at home!

Then I thought, (while not wanting to tell anyone as I didn't want them worrying) that I could hear my inner voice shouting, "This is just not right, get it checked."

So, the first thing I did on the Monday morning was to telephone my GP. I made an appointment, then went and had it checked out.

All the while I was hoping it may have just been something hormonal, and nothing to worry about. Right? Wrong!

My GP examined my breast and asked me many questions and then he unfortunately confirmed that he had felt that there was a lump. So, he then went on to advise me he would need to refer me to the hospital.

Oh great, more worrying and waiting...

How do you tell your sons that their mum has found a lump and needed further tests?

I was so worried for them, it was so wrong on many levels, I should always be here and be able to stay positive for my lads.

Mamma bear must be so strong to protect her young, yet here I was, a weak, bubbling mess, not knowing what was going to happen.

Then, the next stage I had to undergo were;

Examinations (Boobies constantly fondled)

Mammograms (squashed booby time)

Ultrasounds (cold sticky gel)

Biopsies (ouch)

Scans (I never knew just how many different scans there are)

Blood tests (I still don't like needles)

Checking my weight (never daring to look myself)

My Temperature (I am either hot or cold)

Various other tests followed.

The first time while having an ultrasound scan, I laid on the bed with my gown gaping open and my eyes closed wishing I were somewhere else, anywhere but here.

The sonographer left the room and came back in with someone more experienced than her who closely looked at the screen and went on to explain who he was and that he needed to take 4 biopsies. Ouch!

I knew what that meant, they had seen something bad. The biopsies sounded like a machine gun shooting into my breast, leaving me feeling like a pin cushion.
Ouch again!

Once the ordeal was over, the nurse asked me to go back to the examination room. I walked past the other patients, not one was my age, sitting in their robes, some hugging their chests, some staring into space, some reading, (how can they concentrate?) and some probably wishing they could be somewhere else too, all of us giving that sympathetic smile to each other.

A Pocket Full of Hope

As I entered the room, I proceeded to get dressed. There was a knock at the door, the nurse came in followed by the doctor.

Then it got real, I knew she wouldn't have been there if it was good news.

The doctor had his head down, and as I said to him, "It doesn't look good, does it?" he stood still and remained silent for a split second, not even moving to look up at me, yet the nurse looked at me with pitiful eyes.

I guess that's a no then, I thought to myself, not daring to say it out loud, trying to hold back my tears.

(I must remember to buy waterproof mascara.)

You know that feeling when time stands still, your head spins and you feel sick? well that is exactly how I felt. I felt like I was sinking to the bottom of a long endless black well, drowning in my terror.

A Pocket Full of Hope

How could I be in this situation?

Why? Why Why?

Of course, we all think that. I felt so scared.

I didn't want to feel like a victim.

The Breast Cancer nurse looked at me, saying, don't worry, it could be any number of things, and went on to say that they still had more tests to do, but in the meantime to go home, take paracetamol for the pain and then, wait for it, she even joked about trying to relax and have a glass or even a bottle of wine!

Some NHS cocktail that would be!

Is it on prescription? I wondered.

As for relaxing, Relax? How on earth am I supposed to do that exactly!

AND if that wasn't enough, I then had to wait again for the results, 12 days in all, time went very slowly.

Can you imagine the torture of having to wait to see if you have a chance of living or dying? and IF it is cancer, whether it had spread or whether it had been caught in time?

The waiting was so cruel because I couldn't focus on anything except the thought that I might have cancer. I was always having to wait to find out what would happen next.

I have always hated the not knowing, and then dreaded the thought what exactly was to come next, (my imagination was always in overdrive.)

I prayed to the lord.

If the results were to be bad news, would he be here for me, helping me through it all? because I honestly did not feel ready or strong enough for whatever I would have to deal with, by myself, especially knowing I needed to be here for my lads...

PS Jesus never leaves you, but it is always a comfort to pray and have hope.

Whilst waiting for results.

One Saturday, my mum and a couple of my friends, suggested a day out to Leeds, West Yorkshire, for a girly day out, to try and take my mind off what had and what was going to happen.

While we were there, we had a try of some cocktails...

We introduced my mum to the usual names, Strawberry Daiquiri, Mojito, Pina Colada, but the funniest one that made us all laugh the most, was one known as... Japanese Sex!

A Pocket Full of Hope

Wait until she explained to my dad, she'd had Japanese Sex and in Leeds of all places (He's been an avid Manchester United fan all his life. In fact, I think Utd is his life!) ... ha-ha.

I'd have loved to have seen his face with that one!!

Chapter 4

Verdict Day

The results were in...

A queasy uneasy feeling kept doing summersaults inside my belly, let alone what was happening inside my head.

After a couple of weeks of waiting, it was finally time to face my future. I returned back to the hospital along with my mum, dad and my eldest son, and in his words, "Grandma can't hear very well and IF it is bad news, I wouldn't be able to take it all in", so he would be there to listen. How right he was!

Tip

It is advisable to take someone with you if possible, as extra ears are always helpful, and in my case, I did listen, but I just could not take it all in.

A Pocket Full of Hope

The consultant walked in, introduced himself, and made small talk, (all the while I am thinking to myself, just get to the point.)

And then ...

Alarm bells...

Bad news alert...

Drum roll...

Here it comes...

In his serious professional voice, I then heard the dreaded words which I really really didn't want to hear...

"You have Breast Cancer"...

Boom!

It was like an explosion had just occurred, everything went dark, and I found I couldn't hear properly.

The room started to spin, and all the words sounded muffled, just like someone was holding my head underwater.

I then eventually came up for air...

3,2,1 I'm back in the consulting room...

Not that I had physically gone anywhere, just mentally... This can't be true, can it?

I am only 46 years, it's not that old in this day and age is it?

FACT

Do you know one woman every ten minutes is diagnosed with Breast Cancer in the UK?

I have never smoked, never drank a lot of alcohol and I have always eaten healthy, (ok, except for my love of cake.) lol

I have always thought that the right-hand side of my body was stronger than the left side.

(I don't know why; I don't even know if you can have a stronger side.)

My Facts:

I am right-handed.

I wear my bracelets and watches on my right wrist. (Not at the same time though.)

My right booby was used more than the left one while breastfeeding.

Is it so wrong to have cancer in my right breast?

Surely it can't be right, can it?

I always got teased at school for having big boobies.

A Pocket Full of Hope

I complained about shops not having enough choice in pretty coloured bigger sized bras.

But these are MY boobies. Big, yes, with lumps, yes, and now cancer, oh please no, please be wrong.
I wasn't expecting that to happen!

Hocus Pocus I'm brokus!

So why me? Why?

I hadn't felt ill; I had only felt a lump. (The baby lump). That lump soon became a family of lumps. The one I had found turned out to be a cyst, there was also a smaller lump hiding behind it (mummy lump), then the consultant went on to explain that there was another lump, a bigger one, a harder one, to the right hand side of my breast, the one my GP had felt and THAT was the cancerous culprit! (The BIG daddy of all lumps.)

Mr Hutchinson went on to explain I had stage Grade 3 cancer, the faster growing cancer, and that he wouldn't know any more until further tests were completed.

A Pocket Full of Hope

Grade 3 meant it was worse than a 1 and 2. He told me I would need further tests, and one of the tests was to check if it had spread to my bones through the lymph glands.

Spread? Oh, my word now something else to worry about!

Mark 5:36*
Do not be afraid, just have faith.

Now this shit had just got real. It gave a new meaning to shit spreading, I'll tell you that for sure, believe me.
I was petrified!

The consultant was so calm and logical, so professional, well he would have to be, wouldn't he? Silly me.
He then went on to say he wanted to "throw everything at it".
Oh, shit, another thought in my head.

I was going to have an operation, known as a lumpectomy, and possibly another operation, if it had spread.

Lymph Node Removal, Chemotherapy, Radiotherapy and then medication for 10 years would also follow.

Wow! Not much to deal with and go through then...

I am surprised my hair didn't go grey in an instance, right there in the room because of shock!, not that it would matter as he went on to say which treatment he thought would be the best for me, and undergoing chemotherapy would make all my hair fall out, so then I thought, well, going grey was nothing to worry about, I wouldn't have it for long then would I? and compared to everything else I seem to have to deal with.

So once again I would have to wait for more appointments.

Mum says I need a season pass for all the appointments at the hospital.

Some people have holiday homes as their 2nd home, but not me, mine is the hospital!

A Pocket Full of Hope

I was sat there in the hospital and suddenly a thought appeared. I remembered I had bought a pair of Pink Limited-Edition Breast Cancer UGG Boots, the year before, and here I was being told I now have Breast Cancer!

I could have easily booted the ass out of those boots on hearing my diagnosis!

How Ironic eh? I didn't really feel 'in the pink' at that that moment in time.

I wasn't usually good at waiting, I was an impatient patient, having to learn quickly, I wasn't in control of any of this, it was out of my hands, and well, I needed this disease out of my body and pronto!

To find out the cancer was Grade 3, fast growing AND it had also spread to my nodes, was not what I had expected, I wasn't prepared for any of this.

There again, to be honest, who would be? Certainly not moi!

A Pocket Full of Hope

My 1st thought was, am I going to die?
What about my three lads?

Silently the tears came.
(where are all the tissues, when you need one...
or in my case, a full packet, forgetting I had some in my pocket), then as if by magic the doctor passed me a tissue, or was it two? Anyway, they soon disintegrated into a wet soggy mush only fit for the bin.

And so, he went on to finish what he needed to discuss and then explained, in an idiots way for me to comprehend, while I just sat there, with my head all messed up, not knowing what to say, while my salty tears flowed fast out of my eyes and down my face, onto the bed, like a rushing waterfall.

I glanced up, looked in the direction of my mum and son who were sat across from me and suddenly I felt so upset for them.

More tissues please…
I should get shares in Kleenex balsam soft tissues.

Psalm 18:6*
In my distress I cried out to the lord.

Psalm 91:6*
Do not dread the disease that stalks in darkness.

Eventually I pulled myself together (well just a little bit) even though I was shattering into thousands of pieces on the inside, (ok, a slight exaggeration there, but it did feel like it at the time.)

My adrenaline triggered my flight mode giving me an energy rush to run away and 'hide' from all this, yet my noradrenaline created my fight response, readying myself for this battle on the front line against cancer, The Big C against little me! and to prepare the ammunition, tanks, guns, soldiers, ready to win the victories along the way, and to 'seek' out all the help I needed.

It gives a new meaning to hide and seek, I can tell you!

A Pocket Full of Hope

I was to take small steps each day after hearing this devastating news, yet that day, I honestly wanted to take flipping giant BIG steps, to enable me to run out of the hospital right there and then but knowing I couldn't really run.

I needed to stay and listen to the seriousness of this bad news, to be a big girl while wearing my BIG pants, and due to the fact if I did actually run I would honestly be out of breath, needing my inhaler, and even worse, ending up peeing myself!

Me and running are not a good combination, we just do not go together. lol

Walking out of the hospital that day, I then had to break the news to my dad, (he wanted to wait outside), oh boy, it broke my heart, poor dad, my rock, a man of few words, yet so strong.

How the heck he managed to drive me home first and then himself and mum with that bombshell just dropped on them I will never ever know or understand.

A Pocket Full of Hope

Upon leaving the hospital grounds that day it was like I had taken a wrong turning on the road, got lost on an unfamiliar side street and went round the roundabouts too many times, not being able to stop, hitting a dead end and not even being sure if there was even a detour.
All in my head of course.

(Speaking hypothetically as it was dad who was driving.)

As for me, I am not even safe driving a bumper car.

The body is like the shell of a car, our spirit and soul are the car engine, turning over, ticking along, while enabling us to keep moving.

I thought I was a classic, but now I felt like I was turning into an old banger. My back end is still fine, it's just a shame it is the headlights that are dodgy, not exactly shining full on 100%.

Refuelling with Gods words and my medication is like the fuel being pumped into a car from the petrol station.

I wanted to do an emergency stop, braking so hard to try and stop this evil disease in its tracks, yet, at the same time wanting to accelerate so quickly, to get through and then past this dreaded illness.

I wouldn't even care about a speeding ticket!
If it meant I could get on the right road, the road to recovery.

I prayed to see the right signs...

Amber, Am I ready...
Green for go, not Red to stop.
Just like the ones on a set of traffic lights.

Isiah 60:22*
At the right time, the lord will make it happen.

All experiences we must face, as we journey through our tough times, all the roads we take, move us nearer to our destiny.

"Being lost is a way of finding yourself" ...

I can't remember where I read this, but it has struck a chord with me ever since.

Do you know people with cancer are no longer the same as before? Well, certainly not me anyway.

When I was diagnosed, it was like I was unexpectedly hit with a lightning bolt and blinded by the light.

I found I couldn't see properly, I was stunned, I felt I was plunged into darkness, and not quite ever being able to reach the light. The lamp had well and truly blown its light bulb!

A Pocket Full of Hope

Going through cancer was like I was a dimmer switch, starting off in a black, dark, dull, bleak room, then finding myself getting lighter and brighter as I turned the dial of my journeys switch.

Hearing the word Cancer is a very scary, panicky feeling, everything was in slow motion, everyone and everything else was moving so fast, and I wasn't in control, I couldn't put a stop to any of it.

How can you want something to slow down, to have time to take it all in, yet at the same time, wishing it could go faster, to hurry up so I could get through it all?

It was so unfair, the cries from my heavy heart, (A bit dramatic I know) tears falling from my eyes, down my cheeks, onto my pillow, night after night, wrapping my duvet snugly around my broken diseased body, needing 'that' kind of hug, for reassurance, to comfort me.

A Pocket Full of Hope

"Courage does not always roar. Sometimes it is the quiet voice at the end of the day whispering, "I will try again tomorrow". - Mary Anne Radmacher

And so, it still went on...

What followed were 2 Operations:

A Lumpectomy
(Which I ended up staying in hospital for 4 days, instead of overnight.)

Followed by,

A Sentinel Node Removal
(That time I ended up staying in hospital for 10 days due to complications.)

I am sure they had a party once I eventually left.

A Pocket Full of Hope

I also had to have various treatments;

Chemotherapy, which included 2 different types, along with 6 sessions, 3 of each type, which included different side effects.

Radiotherapy (15 sessions) which also included by courtesy of the NHS, 3 tiny tattoos.

So now I can always play dot to dot around my booby if I ever get bored…

Medications (so many meds I thought the staff were kindly giving me a Goody Bag to take home, but no, it was a cocktail full of medications instead, oh! yippee!)

Then endless appointments.

It can get quite confusing, but just remember the 3 W's…

Where, When and What for.

A Pocket Full of Hope

Examinations, which included;

Bra off

Boobs falling to my knees...

(Need arms like an orangutan or Mr Tickle to reach mine)

Gown on (I always put mine on the wrong way around, you'd think I would have learned by now, but no!) Doh!

Doctors hands, take note, they are sometimes warm but beware they can be cold too... brrr!

Blood tests, (so many, and I don't think Dracula would even be bothered to come near me, if he was still alive.)

Scans, (I can't remember how many, but I am sure they have zapped my brain cells once too often.)

Numerous side effects and scars...

Scars are someone else's sign of hope.

"Behind every scar is an untold story of survival".

So very true, I say.

While going through tough times = Not at all easy, it is no fun when you are in it for the long run, but it is doable.

What choice did I have?

Am I weak or strong?

Do I just give in or try my hardest and fight?

I think we all know the answer to that.

Cancer is the devil, it steals your identity, it drags you down to the endless pit of despair and you no longer know who you are.

Getting through cancer is totally different to getting over it! It is a difficult pill to swallow, it got stuck in my throat, and I found it hard to breathe.

It takes mental strength to go through treatment, knowing what it does to your body, and how ill you're going to be while ironically trying to make you well.

It is so physically and mentally exhausting. Please rest when you can, and don't be too hard on yourself.

Dealing with the 'BIG C' is like grief and loss at the same time. I found it very emotional on all levels, it is so very hard, it is just not fair, yet once again I had to wear my big girl pants to deal with it all, full on, and even though I have never actually heard the words that I am fully cancer free, I still to this day try to keep the faith, praying it never returns..

Am I really free of cancer? never to return?

It is all so very scary and worrying but I am still trying to be positive...

I am positive I don't like cancer!

I am positive God will heal me.

A Pocket Full of Hope

I had cancer but it didn't fully have me.

God is not done with me yet.

Isaiah 53:5*
By his stripes I am healed.

I do not know what my purpose in life is, maybe it is writing this book to help myself and, more importantly, to help others, but I will keep on trying, and one day I just may find the answer...

After all God loves a trier doesn't he?

I am now on medication for at least 10 years. Tamoxifen (known to some pink ladies as Tamoxibollox) was prescribed for the first 5 years and now I am on Letrozole, both have different side effects.

PS why isn't there any side effects that say...

May cause extreme sexiness? ha-ha.

A Pocket Full of Hope

So, if the medication, along with God's help, and the medical staff, will help keep me alive and stop the cancer from coming back, as well as the loving support from my family and friends, then I shall say that I am one happy lady, fighter and cancer warrior.

Ps I'm no quitter!

Fact:

October is BC Awareness month.
But for a survivor, it is every single day!

The worst part of cancer? Hmm, let me think...

Cancer has changed my outlook on life. It also changed my life because it threatened it like the big bully of the monster it really is.

Nothing is nice about it. I did get through the difficult times, some days were better than others, sometimes I doubted myself if I could ever get through it all but guess what? Hey, I am still here and smiling!

A Pocket Full of Hope

When I was diagnosed, I cried, and I cried again when I told it was stage 3, fast growing. I also cried again when I was told it had spread to my nodes.

I cried and cried again, never running out of tears.

When I was told I would have to have chemotherapy, more tears flowed.

Pauls grandad used to say, "cry more and you will pee less", well, it didn't work for me. Lol.

I was so upset about the thought of having to lose my long hair.

Stupid really because I should have been telling myself it is all the treatment that I need to help save my life!

Luke 6:21*
God blesses you who weep now, for in due time you will laugh.

A Pocket Full of Hope

And yes, I am so blessed and very thankful to God, the NHS, the Consultant, Surgeons, Doctors, Nurses & Breast Cancer Nurses, all in their angel roles, for all they did to help me. Some will still continue to do so.

For me, the worst part of cancer is the fact that no matter what I have gone through and dealt with, both physically and mentally, it is never really done with, at times I feel there is no miracle cure.

I can only keep praying and putting my faith in God.

I never ever thought cancer would happen to me and I never understood the brutality of the battle until I went through it myself, all the while praying to win the war.

2 kings 20:5*
I have heard your prayers and seen your tears; I will heal you.

A Pink Poem

"This little pink ribbon placed upon this page is a gift I give to you
I merely ask that you pass it on please send it to a friend or two
The ribbon is love and the ribbon is prayer
And it honours those who are gone
It cries for a cure to cancer while the frenzied race goes on
It calls to brave crusaders and asks that we all unite
To battle against the evil foe and on and throughout the night
The little pink ribbon placed upon this page is known across each land
It is the symbol of love and courage, of a kind and helping hand
It unites us as people, and it soothes our sorrowed hearts
It fills our souls with kindness with the message that it imparts".

A Pocket Full of Hope

I always embrace any good news and I always thank the lord after every check-up and follow up appointment until the next time, and the next...

Many times, while attending my appointments, the nurse called my name and then looked straight at my mum instead of me, as if she were the patient!

Err hello, I'm here, it's me!

But do you know what?

I'm so glad it wasn't my mum having to go through all that crap!

Praise the lord.

Chapter 5

Airedale General Hospital Chemotherapy

One time during my chemotherapy session the nurse advised me that it is better not to wear coloured nail varnish, (I had bright pink on at the time) due to having to check my nails, as the treatment can affect them, "clear is better" the nurse suggested...

Well, I like bright colours, especially pink, I think plain is so boring and that is just not me, so I found myself compromising, the week after I walked into Oncology with... wait for it...

Clear, sparkly glittery, shiny nails!

Nothing will ever dull my sparkle!

A Pocket Full of Hope

Having chemotherapy just wasn't for me.

I had quickly decided, while standing there at the door, taking a deep breath and not wanting to move.

But then I eventually bravely made the small footsteps into the dreaded Chemo room.

Every time, I did keep going back, I went for all the sessions, but only because I really needed to.

Endless times spent hooked up to drips, tubes, needles, syringes, bags, wires etc.

Being administered different medications, which were pumped right around my body, flushing me out ready for the cocktail of drugs.
One which I could feel going in, it was a rushing, tingling sensation, which was very strange, it even gave the effect that felt like I was peeing myself! What an awful sensation that was!

Ps I still checked my knickers just to be sure!

A Pocket Full of Hope

"Don't worry if you pee pink", the nurse had said, "that is another side effect".

It was true, I checked that as well!

Then there were the machines that kept beeping, and every so often an alarm would go off, (I'll name that tune in one...lol) announcing the bag was empty and needed changing, with not even a designer bag in sight!

The portable drip stand I had attached each time for treatment, became like a new puppy, always by my side, with me, following me around. Just a bit too attached for my liking!

Then the toilet training started...

Going to the toilet was a nightmare, I kept getting the wires trapped under the wheels, the stand kept twisting around the wires and tubes when it moved, I was in a right muddle.

(Could have been worse, it could have been a puddle!).

How was I supposed to pee easily with the tubes stuck in my hand, while I was holding onto the stand, all the while I'm trying to pull my knickers down one handed!!

I'm aware this may be too much information and my apologies if I have left that image in your head.

But I do think us pink patients need to be prepared for these things.

(Not that I was ever a qualified Girl Guide or Brownie as a child, prepared for every event, because I only lasted one day! don't ask! Lol.)

During another of my chemotherapy sessions, the nurse asked what I fancied to drink, and my answer, after thinking for a nano second, was that I fancied an alcoholic drink.

(By the way I have not drank alcohol since my diagnosis.)

A Pocket Full of Hope

I was only joking with her. I then followed my answer with, preferably in a fancy glass or even put directly into the intravenous bag, which, by the way, was hung on the pole looking sorry for itself, with the tube there reminding me it was stuck painfully in my hand.

I wasn't bothered which option, I replied, with a cheeky grin on my face, it might just numb the pain.

So, then, while turning to look right at me, she replied with a straight face...

"I meant tea, coffee or orange squash" and maybe a biscuit!

Oh, my Lord...
Please give me strength, and while you're at it, give the nurse a humour transplant, so I can at least try to get through these chemo sessions without my jokes dying...

Oh well, at least my mum saw the funny side.

I wondered how long it would be before I was told off...

A Pocket Full of Hope

Thankyou lord that I didn't get detention there!! The hours were long enough as it was thank you very much!

PS I found during my research, (ok, I really meant while I was attending my sessions), that there are 2 types of nurses.

One type are the cancer angels, so helpful, smiling, kind, caring, pleasant, comforting...

The other type is...

The 'Miss Trunchbull' dressed in a nurse's uniform, just to fool you, while having a face like a bulldog chewing a wasp.

The, how on earth can you be an actual nurse?

Come on, seriously are you in fancy dress for the day? Only this isn't funny!

A Pocket Full of Hope

Surely, they must be working in the wrong place.

I needed laughter not misery while going through those tough sessions.

And so, if you've never met one of the latter types, well, what can I say?

Lucky you!

The Dreaded Cold Cap

The first time I was offered the cold cap...

Now as much as I like having a laugh trying on different hats, this was no joking matter, not only did I look stupid once it was on, (I'm so glad at the time my lad didn't take any photos) I was so upset, but now I can laugh at myself knowing how I really looked.. lol

It didn't take me long to say, "get it off NOW"!
I'm not a celebrity but get me out of here!

Talk about brain freeze, in fact that's an understatement.

I think I've only just now thawed out...

I am sure some of my brain cells are still frozen!

So, I concluded, and very quickly, that it wasn't for me, I would just have to accept that I would have to lose my lovely long hair, all while hoping it wouldn't take too long for it to grow back...

Chapter 6

Hair today, Gone tomorrow...

When I brushed my hair, it fell out. In big clumps, not just a few strands.

It fell out in the shower; it fell out into my food. (Nothing should be allowed to put me off eating.)

This was one of the most upsetting stressful experiences for me. It was so traumatic and terrifying.

If I wore a hoodie, the inside of it would be covered in hair when I took it off. It was all over the house, the carpets were covered.

I wished I had a good strong Dyson to suck it all up, not that I had much energy to clean properly anyway.

It also took me longer to clean up the hair in the shower than having the actual shower! How bad was that?

A Pocket Full of Hope

I had long hair, which I hated the thought of getting it cut shorter, just for it to then fall out in clumps so soon after, and ever so quickly.

My brother, Miles, joked that when the time came that I would lose all my hair, at least I would look more like our dad, for once, instead of our mum. Ha-ha the cheek! But he was right.

I did lose all my hair, well, I should clarify that it wasn't actually 'lost', because so much had fallen out on its own accord.

(What a traitor for leaving me) and of course the rest was shaved off.

I honestly did try to think of a positive side to it...

On the plus side, at least I would save money on hair products i.e. shampoo, conditioner, mousse and spray.

Never mind wash and go, it was wash and gone for me.

A Pocket Full of Hope

I was sad that my hairdryer and straighteners were being made redundant, to be put away in the basket, knowing it would be a long long time before I would need to use them again.

And yet, I was right I wouldn't be able to use them, but wrong in the fact they were going to be redundant, to be put away and were to be out of use.

Let me explain, my sons' friends came over to our house on a weekend, and always stayed a while before going on their lad's night out.
While there one friend would get ready, and guess what?

He asked me if he could borrow my hairdryer and straighteners to 'do his hair'. There he was, with long blonde hair, and there I was, with not a strand of hair on my head! Priceless!

How ironic!

That gave me a good laugh, I still chuckle about it to this day.

A Pocket Full of Hope

So many times, I have heard the words...

"It's only hair" It will grow back.

Yes, I know, thanks for the reminder!
(Another thought in my head, I couldn't say out loud.)

But it is MY hair, I've lived with it all my life, from being born with a mass of dark hair to now.

I just wanted to shout out, but of course I have never shouted out anything, from the day of getting my diagnosis, through treatment or even now, I just couldn't get the words that were screaming in my head out of my mouth, it didn't feel right to shout so I kept my thoughts quietly captive.

Please allow me to still be upset and understand what it is like to have no hair. I found it totally devastating.

It is a reminder of who I am and not who I was, and besides vanity, I looked ill, I was a cancer patient. Enough said! Harsh, I know, yet true!

I also saved on razor blades as I didn't have to shave anywhere else on my body. Ooh goody, I found an advantage of chemotherapy!

I was then offered the choice of a hat, scarf or wig.

Now as much as I like coloured, patterned scarves...

I did NOT like the ones for my head.

No way was I ever going to wear one, scarves are to wear around my neck only, and anyway, I wasn't into the fortune teller look, with or without the earrings!

PS No offence to any cancer patient who wear scarves, they just were not for me.

"I hate those scarves; they make me look like I have cancer" I cried.

Mum replied, "but love you do have cancer," bless her.

A Pocket Full of Hope

Yes, I know I have cancer, I just didn't want to look like I had it! (Another thought in my head, and once again not actually shouting it out loud.)

My son kindly gave me his football beanie hat, which I wore around the house and to his football matches, but I only went on my good days.

My mum bought me a black, sparkly, woollen hat. Posh eh? which I adorned for my appointments, until I had chosen a wig. Yes, I was sparkling, but only just.

My youngest son was brilliant, he was the one who went through my cancer the most, living with me through it all.

He was the first to see my bald head, well, only after myself and my friend who had shaved all my hair off.

A Pocket Full of Hope

It takes some balls to show a bald head, balls I didn't have, so I admire anyone who can go out in public without hair, hats, scarves or wigs.

I will never forget that night, while others were out celebrating bonfire night.

I was commiserating. All my hair being swept up off the floor to be put in a bin bag...

And I might add, which was the only thing that went out that night, not me.

There were no sparklers in sight, the only fireworks I heard that night was one of those high-pitched screamers, which in fact was my own voice inside my head, screaming...

Why me?

Chapter 7

Wig Wham, Thankyou Ma'am

The day came to go look and try on some wigs.

It was a day of mixed emotions...

Sad that I had to have this appointment in the first place! (damn you cancer, damn you chemo, and damn you hair for leaving me.)

Yet I was happy I had the chance to be able to buy one, just so I didn't have to go out in the public with a bald cold head. Not that I had the confidence to dare to do that anyway.

I did try to laugh and joke about how I looked when trying on all the wigs. There were short, medium and long ones, with different colours and styles, but inside I just wanted to cry.

A Pocket Full of Hope

In the end I decided on a wig that resembled the nearest to what my natural hair style and colour had been, giving me just a little sense of holding on to my old self before breast cancer took over.

It was a godsend that wig, I could get up in the morning, get showered and dressed then just pop it on and hey presto! I had hair again!

I could wash it in baby shampoo, then let it drip dry. Thank goodness no one saw THAT hanging in my bedroom, what a sight it was!

It came with a stocking cap, which I had to put on my head first, to keep it my wig in place, not a sexy look I can tell you, I looked like I was wearing one of Nora Batty's wrinkled stockings tied in a knot on top of my bald head!

My Hairdresser Joanne was ever so kind because overtime my wig would become a bit tatty on the ends, just like real hair really, apart from it just didn't grow.

Any way whenever I walked into her salon, she would trim the ends to tidy it up for me. (And free of charge, what a bonus, bless her.)

She is such a good friend and hairdresser.

So, I would like to take the opportunity to say thankyou Joanne and all the staff at Liberty Lounge, Keighley, West Yorkshire. You made me feel just a little more 'normal' under the circumstances.

I was also given one of those polystyrene model heads (my lad wanted to draw funny or should I say rude things on it lol) so I could place the wig it on when not in use to keep its shape, yet many times I just hung the wig on the bedpost at the bottom of my bed.

Bet you never thought of decorating your bed like that did you? ha-ha.

A Pocket Full of Hope

I looked like I was ready for Halloween (even cobwebs and dust were included.)

One time, my cousin messaged me with an offer to arrange a night at the local golf club to shave his own hair, to raise money, so I could buy a wig.

Bless him, how sweet and thoughtful that was.

I politely declined as I had already bought one, and after being bald myself and not through choice, I couldn't bear the thought of him having to lose his hair, especially by his own choice, when he didn't really have to.

I will never forget his lovely offer though. I was so touched by his kindness.

Thank You so very much Rick, you don't realise how much your offer meant to me.

A Pocket Full of Hope

In time my hair did start to grow back and at one stage my son felt the top of my head, gave it a rub, and said "you're like a tennis ball"! ha-ha ok, so he got me to laugh at that, nice one son.

Eventually my hair grew back, surprisingly the same colour, but it did have a different texture. I had always had straight hair before breast cancer, but it grew back with slight curls, which I honestly didn't mind at all.

(Another bonus, no need for the curling tongs☐).

I was just so happy to see it finally growing back.

Chapter 8

The C Word

On a serious note I soon lost myself after my diagnosis. Who I was, Who I am.?

Cancer isn't a before and after event, it's part of the continuum that is my life.

I feel a different person now than who I was before cancer, (yes, I'm still a wife, daughter, sister, mum, aunt, cousin, niece, nanna and even that little girl lost inside.)

I am so happy and grateful for knowing I am so blessed, I've still got my new life to live, for how long I don't know, I do know I'm not ready to go to heaven just yet, that's for sure!

But, when the time does come, I believe that death is not the actual end, as I will have eternal life in glory.

Those who never had cancer think we can get over it by waking up one morning and deciding it is now over, just because chemotherapy and radiotherapy and surgeries have finished.
(I am still on medication, attending appointments etc.)

Many have said to me, "My friend/relative had it" I looked them in the face, wondering what was to follow, hoping to hear for that happy ending story of how they beat it and are now enjoying life...

Anything positive to cling to, to grab with both hands and not let go...

"They died" was the reply. Oh, right, thanks for that! NOT!

That was so not what I needed to hear.

No one should have to go through cancer, it is so evil.

Just because I have silenced a memory does not mean I am free of it...

A Pocket Full of Hope

In my mind it is always there, filed in a compartment within a never-ending storage cabinet. Never completely over, you push it to the back, and Hey Ho, up it pops right to the front...

Let me tell you it never seems to go away...

Especially when Satan rears his ugly head...

John 10:10*
The devil comes to Steal, Kill and Destroy...

Do not let him! Fight, Fight, Fight! It is your right.

I have never had much self-worth, from being put down, made to feel inferior, to have been told things deliberately knowing that it would upset me. I felt like I was weighted down with feelings of uselessness, and I was of no value to anyone.

When told on a regular basis, you start to believe they are true, but I now know all these are lies, even from Satan, to affect my way of thinking, to try to destroy me.

Never let him or others control your thoughts. Live the one life you have in a happy positive way, God has got your back, he'll protect you, if you let him.

PS Don't ever blame yourself.

Many times, I have asked myself, is the cancer because of this or that, and not knowing, only to deal with yet another battle ongoing in my head.

There are some questions I have about why I had cancer and yet I know I will never get the answers for them, so I came to accept that and stopped worrying about it.

Philippians 4:6-7*
Do not worry about anything; instead, pray about everything.

With radiotherapy next I could not quite bring myself to celebrate the end of chemotherapy just yet, especially knowing I had more struggles to come...

Bradford Royal Infirmary (BRI)

Appointments here consisted of bone scans and various injections of radioactive substances.

I had to go to the Nuclear Department (I was quite alarmed by this, but it wasn't as bad as I thought, even though my 'scanxiety' levels were quite high.)
I am such a coward at times.

Some blue dye was injected into me, before my scan, so any cancer cells would show up in the lymph nodes in case that the cancer had spread. (Which unfortunately we now know it had.)

The dye helps the surgeon see where it is so it's easier to find.

I was also informed by the nurse that some patients go a shade of a bluey green colour due to the dye.
That's all I needed, to look like a cross between a Smurf and Shrek!

And yes, my breast did go that colour, a strong mixture of blue and green, and not just a tiny bit in a pretty pastel colour. Typical! Ha-ha.

Upon arriving at the hospital, it didn't help that, as I approached and walked towards it, it looked so dull and dismal from the outside, not yet knowing what the inside had in store.

Walking in through the main entrance, the first thing I saw was a chair, placed on its own, in the corridor, with a big sign labelled right across it saying...

'Condemned'.

Oh, my days, that made me laugh, as I could relate to that the poor chair lol.

Having the scans also included being able to use my very own radioactive patients' toilet...

My very own special throne! Aren't I special lol?

St James' Hospital
Radiotherapy

Travelling to the hospital was so tiring and draining. Every day for 15 days certainly took it out of me, and I am sure dad too, as he was the one driving.

The drive also took longer than the actual treatment!

Also, the journey always seemed longer due to my dads' radio being constantly "stuck" on Talk Sport!!

I don't think he knew the radio had other channels available…
Or maybe he did! Thanks for that dad, Not! lol.

Arriving at the hospital, became a guessing game, how many spaces were available today? more or less than yesterday? Dad usually won, as per...

Clever Colonel (PS, he looks just like Colonel Saunders, KFC, hence his nickname.)

A Pocket Full of Hope

On first walking into the main entrance, I thought, what a lovely bright, light, airy, pleasant place to be...

Until I found out that to reach the Radiotherapy Department, involved me getting into the lift and going down to the basement! Down and down I went to the deep dark pit, then the doors opened, and it was like stepping out into a rabbit warren!

On the first day it was explained to me that I had to have 3 tattoos, tiny little blue dots, one between my breasts and one on the side of my rib cage and another under my boob (which were needed for guides.)

This surprised me, but I had to go along with it. I didn't feel them, but it was weird that I now had these marks on me forever.

Thinking about it, I should have asked if they could have been pink instead of blue…

Oh well, they now join my body along with my other tattoos, consisting of an angel, the word "Believe", flowers and butterflies.

I think it is known as body art, though that is not how my mum would describe them, she doesn't like tattoos, Oops).

To this day, I still sometimes look down at the dot at the top of my breast, and think I've got a spot, but it's just a constant reminder of the cancer, a tattoo of the devil's mark! Which tried to kill me.

My Interesting Fact:

I think the butterfly represents my life, like a caterpillar going through pain, pushing through its cocoon, for then to emerge, transformed, with the freedom to fly.

It also represents rebirth, change, hope and life.

It is the symbol of resurrection.

Butterflies have a big significance to me. (Another story).

I also think they are so delicate, and pretty.

Yes, I am very girly.

There was also a chance as the radiation continued that my skin would become red and sore, but by making sure to use the cream provided everyday it should help minimise the damage. The nurse told me, "she would check it at each session, and she could provide burn dressings if it got worse".

I was to avoid wearing a bra with an underwire and if possible, not wear one at all.

Well let me tell you, that is one mighty challenge when, if you're like me having big boobies.

They hang down by my knees without a proper bra! (no exaggeration needed, honestly.)

I felt so conspicuous, awkward and uncomfortable without one, so in the end I just removed the wire from my old bra and used that instead.

Well it wasn't like I was doing a fashion parade was it?

Tip

If you ever feel a stabbing pain in your breast, check first that it isn't a loose wire in your bra sticking into you, before getting checked out by a professional, as it saves on the embarrassment, (I know because it happened to me). Doh!

I must admit the Radiotherapy treatment, experience and side effects were better than chemotherapy, but it did take a lot out of me, it was so exhausting.

Some of my side effects:

I still suffer badly with insomnia and fatigue.

I lost weight with chemotherapy, (yippee).

Gained weight; (boohoo) due to steroids, other medications, oh, and not forgetting the cake, oops!

A Pocket Full of Hope

I had numerous white blood cell count checks which plummeted to the depths of hell to make me even more susceptible to every germ going.

Which is why you are advised not to go to crowded places, i.e. supermarkets, stadiums etc. (Hello, and welcome to the world of online shopping).

I felt dizzy and nauseous. Oh, how I hate feeling and being sick, urgh! And on top of that my mouth was as dry as a camel's backside in a sandstorm.

It even brought on early menopause. (On the plus side, oh great, no more periods for me! on the downside, more side effects to try and cope with.)

The lymph node removal operation also included inserting tubes, running out from my wound. These drained the fluids into a bag and were removed after a few days.

It became a guessing game between the nurses and me of how much fluid had drained into the bag each day. Gross eh?

A Pocket Full of Hope

Can you tell I got bored easily while staying in hospital?

Side-effects of this included, pain, swelling, bruising, stiffness and reduced movements.

During my stay in hospital, having to lay flat in bed was also a challenge, one I didn't really want to accept, as I prefer being on my side to sleep, but due to the tubes and drip it just wasn't possible. Yet, you can only stare up at the plain ceiling for so long! Zzzzz.

The treatment knocks down your immune system,
(I get knocked down, but I get up again...)

Try reading this without singing that song in your head.

It was all so exhausting, yet every day I made myself get up, out of bed, shower and dress and then go sit or lay on the sofa, with my cosy blanket, my body moulded into the sofa, resembling another cushion. Well, I say a cushion, but with the size of my body, a very large squishy bean bag would be a better description!

It also messes with your head, body and looks.
(My teeth now look like sugar puffs)

My gums have changed for the worse.
(Gum Gum for Dumb Dumb)
Can you guess which film that quote is from?

Then just as I started feeling a little better it was time to go back for more sessions...

"Chemo Brain" Is Real.

After treatment I kept forgetting things. My brain feels slower than normal (whatever normal is lol) I find it a struggle to concentrate for long periods of time or remember things. My brain feels foggy and I know my family and friends laugh at me because they don't really believe me, Hence my nickname Princess Dizzy. I just laugh it off with the old "chemo brain" saying but at times it can be quite frustrating and upsetting.

I still suffer with fatigue, insomnia, and constant pain in my joints and bones.

The chemotherapy gave me a metallic taste, urgh! which I couldn't get rid of, fortunately that went soon after.

I peed and cried pink due to the chemotherapy, and blue, due to the radioactive dye.

I had many other side effects, some have gone, others are still here.

It is like they have attachment issues; they just do not want to leave me and will not go away. They are there like bad toothache, a constant painful reminder.

Having cancer can be like a domino effect, in that you go through it, then some other illness (s) comes along trying to knock you down.

Since my cancer I have also been diagnosed with;

Osteopenia
Asthma
Hypercalcaemia
Hyperparathyroidism

A Pocket Full of Hope

Yet, I will not complain because at least I am still alive and determined to kick all their asses!

And I'm still here, Ta Da!

Everyone has different side effects and different reactions, so do not worry, your Breast Cancer nurse will always be there to offer advice and support, as will your Consultant and Doctor. (So many angels here on earth.)

At every hospital appointment, I always kept an angel keyring in my pocket, not for good luck, just for reassurance I think, while praying to God that everything will turn out ok in the end.

I also decided to keep a tissue in my pocket, whether it was for sad tears or happy tears.

A Pocket Full of Hope

How I wished I could have just stuffed the cancer into my pockets, safely zipping them up, so it wouldn't be able to gruesomely grab onto anywhere else in my body.

I would then proceed to walk right out of the hospital, unzip the pockets, throw it to the ground, and destroy it, while safely knowing it wouldn't come back to continually try to destroy me!

Flipping heck, I think I needed bigger pockets! Ha-ha.

When Chemotherapy and Radiotherapy Treatment Ends.

I honestly expected to feel so happy once treatment was over, maybe it was time to celebrate, but in reality, I felt quite flat. Please don't get me wrong, I was relieved it had ended but my cosy, safety blanket had been taken from me. Suddenly my usual 'cancer' routine, which I had been so used to had stopped, what next? there was a different routine to find. It is still a scary time, all the waiting, even when you receive a letter quoting "No worrying signs".

There are times it still feels like I have a demonic force looming over my shoulder for my whole life. There is always a dark shadow, waiting to invade.

When I wake up in the morning, I still sometimes think about it. When I get a pain or feel ill, I think maybe it's back again. I'm constantly exhausted hoping it won't return, praying that it has gone for good.

A Pocket Full of Hope

I have looked at websites and forums with other people battling cancer and too many times I read that someone has announced that the beautiful lady who always had a smile on her face has "gone to the angels" and I feel so sad. I know people say that no one knows what's around the corner but when you have had cancer, cancer is always lurking around every corner.

I just keep all the fear and thoughts to myself, trying to push it to the back of my mind while getting on with my day to day living.

Reading the words "cancer survivor", gives me mixed emotions, as I always want to add, "for now", on the end, I'm trying to stop the negative thinking, I need to stay positive.

I just keep praying and thanking Jesus.

Once the treatment is over, you slam that door closed, locking it securely, hoping never having to reopen it. Then my faith steps in and reminds me that I am healed. I had cancer, it hasn't got me, it has gone.

Psalm 138:3*
As I Pray, you answer me, and encourage me, by giving me strength.

People expect you to just get on with life, to be back to normal, but believe me, it's not quite as easy as that.

No one tells you how hard it is to get over cancer once treatment has finished. There is still more stress to deal with, you have to alter all expectations, it is not a quick fix, you're in it for the long haul, praying you'll pass with flying colours, to have a safe journey home so to be able to get on with your life.

I wanted to feel normal again after treatment ended, yet at the same time I felt like I'd never be "normal" again, and to be honest I don't know what normal is anymore.

Tip

Remember whatever you go through with cancer it is important to do the 4 R's...

Rest, Relaxation, Recreation, and Recovery.

Your mind and body will thank you for it.

I have changed so much, cancer has changed me, my faith in God has changed me, and so now I am a "new happier normal me" (whatever that is.)

I love to laugh and smile, but as I mentioned earlier one of the cancer treatment side effects has ruined my teeth and gums. I was told it could do that, but I wasn't prepared for just how much it would.

So now I try not to show my teeth as they have moved position, they have bigger gaps in them.

You may call it vain, but I call it lack of confidence.

So, I smile with my lips closed, which now, by the way, just makes my cheeks look even fatter, like I'm storing food in them! (Think hamster) Oh, the joys...

I have scars, both physically and mentally, wonky teeth, (back to the sugar puffs again), thinner hair, and I still need to lose weight.

Yet I am trying to stop giving myself a hard time because I need to remind myself that I have also come through the cancer and there is more to my life than worrying how I look.

1 Peter 3:3*
Do not be concerned about the outward beauty, fancy hairstyles or beautiful clothes.

You should clothe yourselves instead with the beauty that comes from within, of a gentle spirit, which is so precious to God.

A Pocket Full of Hope

In my past I have suffered from being bullied by various people, attacked, lied to, lied about, and controlled.

I have also endured physical and emotional abuse, mind games, heartache, and loss.

I have always felt I was a failure, that I am no good, having no confidence, beating myself up about it all, yet here I am, knowing what I have gone through, I must be ok mustn't I?

I'm not good on self-love, but it's something I'm learning to do.

Whatever bad situation is thrown at us, it affects us all and in different ways. We are not all the same. Give yourself time to heal.

Never lose the fire, passion and fighter that is in you.
Anon

Life is so short, every day is a blessing from God, so try to enjoy it, just don't waste it.

A Pocket Full of Hope

If you've never heard of a lady called Lauren Daigle, then I advise you to search for her music. I came across her work and now have a favourite Christian song, which after reading the lyrics, I can really emphasise with.

You Say

I keep fighting voices in my head that say I'm not good enough
Every single lie tells me I will never measure up
Am I more than just the sum of every high and every low?
Remind me once again just who I am,
Because I need to know
You say I am loved when I can't feel a thing
You say I am strong when I think I am weak
You say I am held when I am falling short
When I don't belong, oh you say that I am yours
And I believe, oh I believe
What you say to me
I believe
The only thing that matters now is everything you think of me

A Pocket Full of Hope

In you I find my worth, in you I find my identity,
Taking all, I have and now I'm laying it at your feet

You have every failure God, and you'll have every victory.

Your worth is found in God, about strength over inner negative voices.

It can help to heal and assure of a victory over struggles, if trust can be placed in the right hands.

Cancer can be so aggressive, treatment is brutal, yet we need to be strong for ourselves, even if we feel weak, be proud to be warriors, the medical teams are not just angels, they are our soldiers, all fighting against this evil enemy. Not just to win the battle, but the war.

Another problem I found I had was the loneliness. I wasn't alone in the sense of having family and friends, but, at times, I did 'feel' alone.

I found myself sequestering away from all, in my comfort zone, my safe place, crying in bed, once again wrapping the duvet around myself, or when I laid on the sofa, wrapping my cosy blanket around me, just like a child, not wanting to be that ill, weak, grown up.

Even when I was admitted into hospital, I felt alone, wishing a member of my family could just be there with me on the days of my operations, but knowing no one was allowed, and even at my age I felt like a little girl needing the comforting loving feeling, a hug that feels like a big soft cosy blanket, that reassurance, all will be ok.

I also had the usual emotions you would expect while being taken down to theatre for my operations.

A Pocket Full of Hope

One time the surgeon came to collect me himself and pushed me in the wheelchair, down from the ward, ready for theatre, which apparently was quite unusual.

(Special treatment for me then.)

Apart from banging both myself and the wheelchair right into the door while trying to go through it!

You couldn't make it up, but it did make me smile and took my mind off what was to come next.

That is something else I don't like, the anaesthetic, the needle and the woozy feeling as you drift off into the land of nod, not being in control, not knowing what was really happening, and then waking up feeling ever so drowsy in the recovery room.
Mind you it is the only time I had a good sleep!

I was lucky, waking up to familiar faces, as my cousins work in the Recovery Department. Thanks Janette and Bev. It really helped me having you both there.

Cancer is also a very lonely place at times. I got lost in my own head. While being diagnosed, in the scanning machines all alone with my thoughts, in bed during the night, again all alone, with no one to talk to or cry beside.

Tip

It can be very isolating, so it is important if you could try to speak or be with someone, even if it is just for a short while, during part of the day, like it was for me, as I found it did help.

I also joined a Cancer Group on Facebook and spoke to Macmillan Cancer Support.

This helped with the feeling that you are not on your own, there are others going through the same or similar experience.

If you have any questions, or just want to rant, people will listen, reply and advise, if needed. Don't be afraid to ask!

Chapter 9

Counselling

I was once referred to a Counsellor, a lovely lady called Pam, who helped me with many issues. We discussed about my cancer, divorce, and attack, amongst other issues and where my mind, thoughts and emotions were to that date.

"Good luck Pam", I thought to myself, the first time we met and chatted about what would be happening in my future appointments. Lol.

Overtime, and credit where credit is due, Pam greatly helped me to move on from these awful, devastating, traumatic events.

She even asked if she could pray with me, so I agreed and the first time she held my hand to pray, I closed my eyes, and the only image I saw and so strongly was the outline of Jesus. Wow! What an experience that was!

A Pocket Full of Hope

I had many sessions with Pam and one time she suggested making a 'bucket' list.

Well, straight away I said no, I couldn't do that, I thought it sounded like I was going to die.

In the end we then agreed to call it a 'Living List' instead.

(In my head the actual words were more like, 'F@@k it List', naughty I know, but once again I was far too polite to say it out loud, sorry Pam, ha-ha).

(By the way, I am still thinking of things to add to the 'whatever' it's called list.)

A few years later, I was so happy and honoured that Pam and her husband Brian accepted our wedding invitation. It was so lovely to see her again and this time as a friend and not my counsellor.

Happy blessings!

Chapter 10

My Family

I have always worried about my family, especially while I was going through my cancer journey, because it is never just me that it affects.

They are still so very supportive, so I need to take this opportunity to say a **BIG** thank you from the bottom of my heart, in all they have done and continue to do for me.

I have not enough words to express my total appreciation for all they do.

I really do love you all. xx

I've also experienced other bad situations in my past. One being, a few years before my cancer, I was badly attacked, which left me with so many physical injuries and mentally, emotional issues, but again in time I overcame them.

A Pocket Full of Hope

I won't go into all the details of the attack, but what I do want to mention is that 3 days before it happened, there was a programme on television about Angels. The, do you believe, do you think you have an angel? etc

Anyway, while I was walking home from work, through the park, (as I did every day), suddenly that programme came into my head, right there in that moment, so I then thought to myself...

I hope I have an angel to protect me if ever I find myself in danger...

Now, people may think I didn't have an angel, due to being attacked, with serious injuries, and yet I honestly think I do have, because not only did I manage to get out of that park, on my own, to get help, despite all my bad injuries, but the CID actually said I was very lucky to survive, as some people do not live after one hit to the head, let alone 3!.

Coincidence or something else?

A Pocket Full of Hope

I think life is so precious, we are precious, not to be hidden away in the darkness of a jewellery box, but to be kept open, sparkling and shining brightly, not just for yourself but for others too.

Looking back on all this, reliving the trauma, the memories, it is so hard, upsetting and painful yet in a strange way, quite cathartic.

It has made me realise at least I am now strong enough to continue to deal with it all, and in the process write about it.

With the ghost of cancer, (despite me always trying to be positive).
It is still lurking somewhere within...

It's just like a bad horror story; frightening and scary, not knowing what's going to jump out in front of you next.

Yet also knowing it's just another chapter of my life, and not the full story, it is not the end...

A Pocket Full of Hope

I just need to keep turning the pages of my life...

Moving forward, whilst praying and thanking God to bless me with a happy ending...

Never forgetting there is always hope, faith and love.

"Love is a feeling, a passion, a deep caring, bringing with it a purpose and a desire to protect from all harm." - Anon

The cancer monster hid inside me, hanging on like the darkest demon sucking my life away for long enough, I had to fight it day after day, month after month, year after year.

It knocked me to the floor but now I'm standing tall, I tell myself I am not afraid of it anymore, I'm facing the light instead of being consumed by the darkness, it will no longer hold power over me.

It has made me want to live my life to the fullest, reminding myself that tomorrow is always a privilege.

"Anything that comes and goes in your mind is not 'yours' they are conditions of the mind. Nothing that comes and goes is 'you'." - Eckhart Tolle

Cancer is so cruel and spiteful and unfortunately sometimes deadly, but there will come a time when it will be defeated, research is ongoing all the time.

I am praying for it to be a distant memory.

Never give up hope.

We will never forget our Pink angels who have been taken too early before us, yet not giving up without a flipping good fight!

What's Next...

I am looking forward to more chapters in my life with my husband, children, and the rest of my family, and for whatever lies ahead in the future, I will deal with, with all my strength, because I have already bravely looked the big bad monster straight in the eyes and I'm so blessed to still be here to tell my tale!

Hallelujah!

I am a WARRIOR.
I'm not perfect but I am WORTHY!
Gracefully broken but beautifully standing.
I am loved by God, my family and friends.
I am ALIVE.
I have been BRAVE!
I choose LOVE and KINDNESS.
It has taken me a long time, not just to realise all this, but to Believe it!

A Pocket Full of Hope

I am proud to be who I am & how far I have come even though I'm still in the process of becoming a better version of myself!

Ps it is not the end...

My wings will have to wait as my story isn't over yet.

Ephesians 5:8*
For once you were full of darkness, but now you have light from the lord.

Present Day

In 2014, I had the blessing of Paul coming into my life. He is such a kind, funny, special man.

Many Years Ago

One day I bumped into an old friend who I had not seen for over 20 years. Little did I know that he was a good friend of Pauls and had been for many years.

A Pocket Full of Hope

Pete mentioned to Paul that he knew someone who would be good for him (and yes, surprise surprise, he meant me!) lol

Another coincidence?

We have since married, with the added blessings of being part of each other's loving family, made complete with 2 adorable puppies, and the recent birth of another grandchild.

Life goes on, and whatever situations we have to deal with, (I know I have other ongoing health issues, flash backs, bad memories, of the attack, cancer, and other trials, traumas etc), yet, in time, I know I will get through them.

I really am so happy and ever so grateful for my extra chances in life.

Honestly, I am so blessed.

Happy endings really can happen!

A Pocket Full of Hope

"The most beautiful people we have known are those who have known defeat, suffering, struggles, loss and yet have found their way out of those depths" - Elisabeth Kibler Ross

Matthew 7 7:12*
Ask and you will receive
Seek and you will find
Knock and the door will be opened for you.

Your prayers can be answered!
It might not be straight away, when you want, need or expect, because it will happen in Gods time.

Maybe things need to change before it happens, never give up, and if it doesn't happen then look within as it just might not be the right thing for you, or maybe you need to change before something better will happen instead. Just keep believing!

A Pocket Full of Hope

And, if you've never read the bible, I am sure, if you take the time to have a look you may just find something that could help you, in anyway, whatever your circumstances. Just like I did.

I would like to mention that at the beginning of my story, I did not own an iPad, electronic notebook, laptop or computer. I wrote this book, first by making notes and then typing them onto a word document, on my phone.

So never think it cannot be done, as I have proved it can be achieved, even if it was a tiny screen I squinted at, while my fat fingers kept hitting the wrong letters.

Eventually I had the Word Document installed onto Paul's laptop to enable me to continue and complete this book.

Just remember...

Never ever quit!

There is always a way!

Luke 1:37 *
For nothing is impossible if you have God.

Cancer is a serious subject, yet I wanted to express the two sides in my book. A lighter hearted side to the heavy going, a happy to the sad, a light to the dark, and the positive to the negative times.

I always try to turn my thoughts around from bad to good, the negative to positive.

PS don't forget to ask your GP or consultant to issue a prescription for positivity, a sense of humour, strength, love and support, because if you're blessed to have these, then this type of medication is a must! And that goes for any illness, I might add.

I honestly do believe that keeping a positive mindset throughout cancer is essential.

I have also just recently had another prophecy, one that is spoken of a "Creative Miracle" ...

"God desires to release creative miracles through my life to others"

So, if it hasn't already happened, then watch this space!

Afterword

It has been such a long hard journey writing this book and as I mentioned at the beginning, if it helps just one person, then I know in my heart it has been worthwhile and I thank God and the NHS Angels for giving me the opportunity to do so.

I have now finished my pocketful of words, and so, **Congratulations.**

You have made it to the end of *A Pocketful of Hope*, with my love in your hands.

I would like to take this opportunity to humbly thank you for taking the time to read my first ever book.

I hope you have enjoyed reading it, and that it has helped you in any way, but if not, please pass my pink journey on, as it may just help someone else.

And now I would just like to finish with sending you all my love and God's blessings, and as my Nana used to say,

Good Night and God Bless.

Elaine J Jeffrey

X

A Pocket Full of Hope

A Pocket Full of Hope is my journey of going through Breast Cancer, with added scriptures, quotes and prayers, that helped me through my devastating diagnosis in 2013, through the sad into happy, dark into light and negative into positive times.

Please send a copy as a gift to someone who has or is going through difficult times with cancer, as it may just benefit them in any way, however small, from reading it.

Or just keep a copy for yourself, the choice is yours.

Thank you, with all my love and blessings.

My steps to Sozo

To make new, to protect, to save, to heal, to preserve, to have faith, to make whole, to love, to make joyous, to have control, to worship, to be made pure; everything good that comes from God...

And she became *Sozo*...

A Pocket Full of Hope

A Pocket Full of Hope